D0913354

A
Child's View
of Grief

Alan D. Wolfelt, Ph.D.
Director, Center for Loss and Life Transition

Cover illustration by Lori Mackey

ISBN 1-879651-00-9

Contents

Preface

A Child's View of Grief is a practical guide for adults who wish to assist bereaved children. Perhaps no greater helping opportunity exists than helping a child whose life has been touched by the death of someone loved.

Without a doubt, communicating with children about death is one of the most challenging experiences adults ever face. It is also one of the most important.

A Child's View of Grief explores a variety of important topics related to children and grief. This guide will help caring adults increase their understanding of how to talk with children about death and grief. There are special sections on Involving Children in the Funeral and Adolescent Mourning.

Introduction

When someone loved dies, children grieve. The most important factor in how children react to the death is the response of the adults who influence their lives. Caring adults—whether they are parents, relatives or friends—can help children during this tragic time. Handled with warmth and understanding, a child's early experiences with death can be opportunities to learn about life and living as well as death and dying.

For parents and other adult caregivers, the first step in learning how to help children deal with death is to become educated about grief. Well-intentioned adults sometimes pass on their own anxieties and fears to the children they are trying to help. Studies show that children often suffer more from the loss of parental support during this time than from the death itself.

Children in our society are referred to as the "forgotten mourners." Children grieve, but all too often they don't get the opportunity to express their feelings openly. This is a situation concerned adults must address. The challenge is to learn how to establish "helping-healing" relationships with children whose lives have been touched by the death of someone loved. When caring adults meet this challenge, children are capable of reconciling grief in healthy ways.

Children and Death: A Historical Perspective

In early America, death was a familiar experience. When several generations of a family lived in the same household, children became aware of aging, illness and death. They watched grandparents grow old. They gathered with other family members when death occurred. Usually, funerals were held in the home.

Under these circumstances, children realized a significant loss had occurred. Along with their parents, they experienced tears and sorrow. Death was something that happened all around them. As a result, they came to know it gradually. For children in early America, death was not a mystery.

Today, children live in a "grief-avoiding" culture. For a variety of reasons, children in the United States often grow up without being exposed to the pain of grief during childhood. Modern medicine, for example, has drastically reduced infant and child mortality and has prolonged life expectancy for the aged.

Families are now also geographically scattered. Deaths occur thousands of miles from home. Even if different generations remain in the same area, the increased use of hospitals and nursing homes reduces the chances that children will witness the aging and dying of their loved ones. Consequently, many children do not have the opportunity to experience the normal grief that accompanies these events.

Ironically, children today are continually confronted by situations where they see that life no longer exists. They find a dead bird in the yard. Their pet dog is hit by a car or they watch TV and see the results of an earthquake or airplane crash. The questions they ask about death grow out of these experiences of daily living. They turn to the adults closest to them for help in understanding difficult questions about death such as, "Will my parents die?" and "What happens to people after they die?"

Parents need to answer these questions openly and in language that children can understand. Being sensitive to a child's needs can make a critical difference in whether the first experiences with death are a helpful or harmful part of their emotional growth. If children are not given honest answers appropriate to their age levels, they often develop distorted attitudes concerning death, dying and funerals. These attitudes, unfortunately, may stay with them for the rest of their lives.

Children Teach Adults About Grief

Children respond to the death of someone loved in different ways. Each response is unique. Rather than prescribing what their grief experiences should be, parents and other caring adults must allow children to be the teachers. In so doing, they will share with adults their personal journeys through grief. Bereaved children have so much wisdom to offer. Adults need only learn how to listen.

Adults should never assume they know exactly how children feel when someone loved has died; or that those in a certain age group will understand death in the same way. Nor should they determine for children when it's time to stop grieving. Instead, children can teach adults what the experience is uniquely like for them.

As students, caring adults need to communicate several important attitudes: respect, acceptance, warmth and understanding. Respect means treating children as separate persons without being possessive or purposely damaging their self-esteem. Acceptance involves supporting them without judging their behavior. Rather than approval or disapproval, acceptance means recognizing that children are unique and need to be acknowledged for themselves.

Another important attitude in a helping-healing relationship is warmth—a demonstration of personal closeness to grieving children. Adults need to remember that two-thirds of all communication is nonverbal. Behavior always speaks louder than words. Tone of voice, eye contact, posture, and facial gestures are a few of the nonverbal cues adults can use to help children teach them about grief. For adults, understanding or being aware of their own experiences with loss might affect their capacity to be emotionally available to grieving children. Adults who are able to separate their own needs from the needs of the children they wish to help make better students. These adults are more able to learn what grieving children have to teach.

With these attitudes, adults can work with children through individual grief experiences, lending a supportive, stabilizing presence.

Dimensions of Childhood Grief

When someone loved dies, children express themselves in a variety of ways. Caring adults need to be aware of these forms of expression and recognize them as natural ways children work through their grief. Twelve dimensions of grief commonly experienced by bereaved children are listed below. This list is not all-inclusive nor mutually exclusive. These grief responses occur in no specific order or progression. Each child's responses are uniquely different.

DIMENSIONS OF CHILDHOOD GRIEF

Apparent Lack of Feelings   Acting-Out Behavior

Physiological Changes   Fear

Regression Behavior   Guilt and Self Blame

"Big Man" or "Big Woman" Syndrome   Relief

Disorganization and Panic   Loss and Loneliness

Explosive Emotions   Reconciliation

NOTE: For a more complete overview of these dimensions see, Wolfelt, A.D. (1983) **Helping Children Cope With Grief.** *Muncie, IN: Accelerated Development, Inc. Phone 303-226-6050.*

Apparent Lack of Feelings

Children often respond to the death of someone loved with emotional shock and an apparent lack of feelings. They can be playing in the yard only hours or even minutes after learning of the death. Rather than being inappropriate, this behavior is a protective mechanism and nature's way of caring for children. It allows them to detach themselves from the pain in the only way they can.

Adults are often confused by this apparent indifference. However, they should recognize it as a child's way of naturally pushing away, at least temporarily, the knowledge that a loved one has died. Adults at this time must be supportive and accept this behavior as a necessary step toward healing.

Adults can also provide opportunities for children to mourn in healthy ways but should never force them to feel something before they are ready for the pain that precedes healing. Just as an adult puts a Band-Aid on a child's physical wound, adults must respect a child's need to temporarily cover up emotional wounds.

Regression Behavior

Under the normal stress of grief, children often return to a sense of protection and security they experienced at earlier times in their lives. This need is manifested in different ways: a desire to be rocked or nursed, difficulty in being separated from parents or requests for parents to do simple tasks, like tying shoes, which children could previously do for themselves. They may also have difficulty in working independently at school. During this time, a child might also need constant individual attention, be suddenly afraid of the dark or talk "baby talk". Regressive behaviors in bereaved children are usually temporary. If children are allowed the freedom to return to simpler, safer times, they will usually emerge from their mourning more competent. Children who are not allowed to regress, however, sometimes bury the pain within themselves.

Regression can happen at any time in the grief experience, but it usually occurs immediately following the death. The efforts of parents and other adults at this time should include providing children a supportive presence that permits them to share their conflicting thoughts and feelings without fear of judgment.

"Big-Man" or "Big-Woman" Syndrome

The opposite of regression behavior among grieving children is the "Big-Man" or "Big-Woman" syndrome. This is apparent when a child attempts to grow up quickly and exhibits adult behavior in an effort to replace the person who has died. This forced maturity can be the result of simply carrying out the instructions of respected adults: "You'll now have to be the man (or woman) of the house."

Although well-intentioned, these persons are unaware of the potentially damaging impact of this message. Sometimes a child unconsciously adopts this syndrome as a symbolic means of trying to keep the one who has died alive. By filling this loved one's role, a child doesn't have to acknowledge the full effect of the loss on his or her life. "Big-Man" and "Big-Woman" behavior in children is sometimes reinforced by grieving adults who find it easier to respond to children at this inappropriate level. In its extreme form, a child literally serves as a replacement for a dead spouse. When this occurs, self-identity and self-esteem frequently are severely damaged.

Adults can take a major step toward preventing forced maturity in grieving children. They can do this by preventing other adults from handing out such trite advice as "You'll have to take care of your mother now that your dad is gone." This kind of comment only results in the development of frustrated or depressed children who are not allowed to grieve in ways appropriate to their ages.

Explosive Emotions

This dimension of grief is often the most upsetting for adults. Parents and others are uncertain how to respond to an expression of complex emotions such as anger, blame, hatred, terror, resentment, rage and jealousy.

Behind these explosive emotions, however, are a child's more primary feelings of pain, helplessness, frustration, fear and hurt caused by the death of someone loved. Anger and other related emotions are natural, intelligent responses by a child in an effort to restore the valued relationship that has been lost.

A child's anger and rage may be directed toward anyone available: the surviving parent, a teacher, friends, God or the world in general. The fact that the dead person does not come back, despite the explosive emotions, is part of the reality testing children need for the eventual healing process. Although confusing for adults, a child's ability to show explosive emotions is healthy. It provides a means of temporarily protesting the painful reality of the loss. Children who either do not give themselves permission to protest, or don't receive permission from others, may turn their anger inward. The result is often low self-esteem, depression, chronic feelings of guilt and physical complaints.

The major role of the caring adult during periods of explosive emotions is to be a supportive stabilizer. Be understanding. Encourage and validate these emotions without judging, retaliating or arguing. Allow children to let go of pent-up emotions. Healthy grief requires that we express, not repress, these feelings in a safe and loving environment.

Acting-Out Behavior

Many children will express the pain of grief through acting-out behavior. After experiencing the death of someone loved, children may have temper outbursts, become unusually loud, initiate fights, defy authority or simply rebel against everyone. Sometimes grades will drop, or the child assumes a general I-don't-care attitude. Older children may talk about running away from home.

For adults, understanding and appropriately responding to this acting-out behavior is often difficult. To establish a helping-healing relationship with children who are demonstrating this dimension of grief, adults need to first examine what causes it. Some of the factors that influence acting-out in bereaved children are:

Feelings of Insecurity. Grieving children naturally experience a sense of insecurity following the death of someone loved. In contrast, acted-out feelings unconsciously provide them with a sense of strength, control and power.

Feelings of Abandonment. When someone

loved dies, children sometimes feel that the person has abandoned them. Consequently, they feel unloved; their self-esteems may be low. Acting-out behavior creates a self-fulfilling prophecy: "See, nobody loves me."

Desires to Provoke Punishment. Unconsciously, grieving children may feel so guilty when someone loved dies that they want to be punished for the death. Acting-out behavior elicits that punishment. The acting-out behavior may even be directed toward trying to get the deceased one to come back. The rationale: "If I'm bad, Dad will have to come back and make me behave."

Desires to Protect Self from Future Loss. By acting-out, or keeping people at a distance, children often try to insulate themselves from feelings of abandonment in the future. They become the ones who control the situation where loss is experienced. Unconsciously, children reason it is better to be the abandoner than the abandoned.

Desires to Externalize Feelings of Grief. Acting-out behavior is often demonstrated in children who have been grieving within themselves but not sharing this grief outwardly. Some adults mistakenly assume children are too young to need to talk out thoughts and feelings about grief. The result — many children grieve but do not mourn. Acting-out is, consequently, a way of saying, "I hurt, too."

For parents and other adults, the key to responding to acting-out behavior is to allow children to teach us what their needs are. By doing so, adults can help children heal the wounds resulting from the death.

Loss and Loneliness

This dimension, feelings of loss and loneliness, is often the most difficult for grieving children. It never takes place all at once and may continue for months after the death. Usually, these feelings begin when a child finally realizes that the person who has died is never coming back.

As children struggle to come to terms with the finality of the death, they may become depressed. This condition is a natural response to their loss. During this time, children may demonstrate a lack of interest in themselves or others, a change in appetite and sleeping patterns, nervousness, inability to enjoy life and low self-esteem. Children are particularly vulnerable at this time. They may become extremely dependent on other persons, possibly someone who reminds them of the person who has died. Caring adults play an important role in helping children grow through this dimension of grief. By communicating in both words and touch, adults can assure children they are not alone in their grief and help them move toward encountering life, living and loving once again.

Reconciliation: The Final Dimension

Reconciliation is the final dimension of healthy grief. While children never get over their grief, they become reconciled to it. At this point, children recognize life will be different without the presence of the person who died. Yet they have a renewed sense of energy and confidence and want to become involved in the activities of life once again.

Adults should never prescribe specific timetables to reach reconciliation. A child will proceed at his or her own pace, depending on age, personality, social environment and relationship to the person who has died. Changes often noted during a child's reconciliation process include:

◆ A return to stable eating and sleeping patterns

◆ A renewed sense of well-being

◆ A subjective sense of release from the person who had died

◆ An increase in thinking and judgment capabilities

◆ An increased ability to enjoy life's experiences

◆ A recognition of the finality of the death

◆ An establishment of new and healthy relationships

Perhaps the most important gain in the reconciliation process is the child's ability to successfully cope with the loss. The child has come to terms with grief and is ready to get on with the business of living.

Reconciliation can best be achieved with the assistance of helping-healing adults who allow children to move toward their grief, not away from it. Children need to know that grief is nothing to be ashamed of.

Even when children reach reconciliation, instances of re-grief may occur. This is natural and is sometimes triggered by a specific holiday or event that reminds them of the person who has died. And while the sense of loss may reoccur, it's softer — the pangs of grief will be less frequent and less severe.

Possibly one of the biggest challenges for any adult is to guide growing children toward this final dimension. The task is often exhausting, not only for children but also for the adults who are helping them. In the following pages, specific skills are identified which will help adults guide children through grief and on to reconciliation.

The Role of Caring Adults When a Death Occurs

How adults respond when a loved one dies has a major effect on the way children react to the death. Sometimes parents don't want to talk about the death. They assume this will spare children some of the pain and sadness. The reality, however, is that children will grieve anyway. To help them through grief, parents need to establish a relationship in which the death is talked about openly. Children need to understand that grief is a natural feeling when someone they love has died.

Children also need confirmation from adults that it's all right to be sad and to cry, and that the hurt they feel now won't last forever. When ignored, children may suffer more from feeling isolated than from the death itself. Worse yet, they feel all alone in their grief.

The first step in establishing a helping-healing relationship is to listen carefully to what children are saying. Allow them to do the teaching. Adults, on the other hand, provide the support, love and understanding.

As children express their feelings about the death, adults need to respond with sensitivity and warmth. Be aware of the tone of voice. Be sure to maintain eye contact. What is communicated without words can be just as meaningful to children as what is actually said. Let children know their feelings will be accepted and that they will not be judged or criticized during this stressful time.

◆

The Importance of Empathy

When someone dies, adults need to create safe environments where children can openly express their grief. To do so, adults must convey empathy and have the courage to become actively involved in the emotional suffering which is a normal part of grief. Empathy means being able to recognize a child's inner feelings — *from the child's point of view.*

Adults convey empathy when grieving children feel understood and supported. To let children know their feelings are understood helps them feel secure, trusted, warm and affirmed. Empathy is the essence of a helping-healing relationship.

The ability of adults to communicate empathy has multiple benefits for children whose lives have been touched by death:

•They are more likely to share deep and personal feelings.

•They feel secure in a trusting environment where they don't feel the need for self-protection or isolation.

•They are able to explore puzzling feelings and grow toward self-understanding and reconciliation of their grief.

While parents may have considerable knowledge about grief, without empathy a helping-healing relationship cannot occur. It is the foundation upon which all other helping qualities are built.

◆

Guidelines for Involving Children in the Funeral

Although children may not completely understand the ceremony surrounding the death, adults need to involve them in the experience of the funeral. This involvement helps establish a sense of comfort and the understanding that life goes on even though someone they loved has died.

Since the funeral is a significant event, children should have the same opportunity to attend as any other member of the family. They should be allowed to attend, never forced. Parents should explain the purpose of the funeral. It's an opportunity to help, support and comfort each other, as well as a time to honor the life of the person who has died.

Funerals provide a unique opportunity for the natural expression of grief and allow those attending to say "thank you" for the privilege of knowing and caring for the person who has died. Most importantly, funerals are also a means of affirming that life goes on even though it is significantly different from when the person loved was alive.

Parents need to keep in mind the following factors regarding children and funerals:

- ◆ While they should be encouraged to attend the funeral, children must feel they have been given a genuine choice.

- ◆ Children need to know ahead of time what they will see and experience at the funeral (flowers, who will be coming, and how long the funeral will last).

- ◆ Children also need to know that the people they will see at the funeral will probably be expressing a wide variety of emotions. They need to know it's natural to cry.

- ◆ Children's first visits to the funeral home should be with only a few people who are especially close to them. This allows children more freedom to react and talk openly about feelings and concerns.

- ◆ Before, during and after the funeral, children need the physical closeness and comfort of parents and other caring adults. Specific words may not be as important as a hug or a hand to hold.

- Adults should anticipate that children may show little, if any, outward sign of grief at the funeral. This apparent lack of externalized mourning does not mean that children are not affected by the death.

- At the funeral, children will be teaching what the death means to them.

- Adults need to be good observers of children's behavior at the funeral and realize that being patient and empathetic is important at this time.

◆

Additional Helping Guidelines for Caring Adults

Be good observers. Don't rush in with ready explanations. It's often more helpful to ask exploring questions than to give quick answers.

- When describing the death of a loved one, use simple and direct language.

- Be honest. Express personal feelings about

the death. By doing so, children have a model for expressing their own feelings.

- ◆ Allow children to express a full range of feelings. Anger, guilt, despair and protest are natural reactions to the death of a loved one.

- ◆ Listen to children; don't just talk to them.

- ◆ Don't expect children's reactions to be obvious and immediate at the time of the death. Be patient and available.

- ◆ Recognize that no one procedure or formula will fit all children, either at the time of death or during the months that follow. Be patient, flexible and adjust to individual needs.

- ◆ Adults must explore their own personal feelings about death. Until they consciously examine their own concerns, doubts and fears about death, it will be difficult to support children when someone loved has died.

◆

Adolescent Mourning: A Naturally Complicated Experience

Each year, thousands of teenagers experience the death of someone they love. As adults do, these survivors grieve (the internal experiencing of thoughts and feelings following a death) but often do not mourn (the external, shared social response to the loss). Unfortunately, adolescents hear messages from well-intentioned adults such as "Keep your chin up," "Keep busy," or "Carry on."

Steve, age 18, is a good example of a grieving teenager who was denied the right to mourn the death of his mother. Finally, three years after her death, he was able to talk openly about the experience. Steve said, "When my mom died, I thought my heart would break, but I couldn't cry." Friends and family told Steve to "be strong" and that he "could take it." For Steve, the result of repressing his grief was a feeling of anger, sadness and isolation.

Obviously, these messages advocating denial prevent Steve or any adolescent from doing the work of mourning. In addition, a number of other factors often make mourning during this period in a teenager's life a naturally complicated experience. These factors include concurrent developmental tasks; sudden, often premature deaths; unique environmental conditions and the potential of conflicting relationships.

Concurrent Developmental Tasks

With the exception of infancy, no developmental period is as filled with changes as adolescence. Consequently, the death of a parent, sibling, relative or friend can be devastating during this already developmentally difficult time. At the time the bereaved adolescent is facing the death, he or she is often experiencing significant psychological, physiological and academic pressures.

Psychologically, one of the most difficult but necessary tasks for a teenager is to leave the security of childhood and begin the process of separation from parents. The paradox is, however, that as adolescents strive for independence, they are still dependent on their families for most psychological and physical needs. The death of a family member naturally threatens the maintenance of these needs.

Because adolescence is often accompanied by awkward physical development, teenagers sometimes feel unattractive. This difficulty with physical self-acceptance makes it hard to have consistently positive self-esteem and affects how teenagers respond to the death of a loved one. Adults need to remember that physical development does not always include emotional maturity. While teenagers may begin to look like adults, they still need consistent and compassionate support—just like children—while they are mourning.

Academic achievement and competition are also complicating factors in bereaved teenagers' worlds. While they are trying to survive the death of someone in their lives, pressure often exists to go to college and even get into the "right college." Struggling with a loss sometimes makes it difficult for them to perceive the value that adults are placing on academics and higher education.

During adolescence, teenagers have a tremendous amount of growing up to do — physically and emotionally. These concurrent developmental tasks make it hard for them to mourn in constructive, healthy ways. Adults need to be aware of these accompanying tasks and encourage bereaved teens to teach them about their grief.

Sudden, Often Premature, Deaths

Many of the deaths that adolescents observe are unexpected and traumatic. A parent dies of a sudden heart attack. A brother or sister is killed in an automobile accident. Or a friend commits suicide. The very nature of these kinds of deaths often results in a prolonged and heightened sense of unreality for teenagers.

The traumatic nature of these deaths is compounded by the very intense relationships teenagers often have with the people in their lives whom they love. Family break-ups often result in teenagers living with grandparents. Even if warning precedes the grandparent's death, the loss is significant and painful.

Most adolescents also have intense relationships with their siblings. There is often competition, rivalry, and components of both love and hate. Should a brother or sister die suddenly, a natural sense of blame or responsibility can occur. Teens also can be extremely close to friends. As when a sibling dies, teenagers need an opportunity to mourn the death of a best friend.

Traumatic deaths make the grief work for teenagers complicated. They sometimes find it difficult to accept the intensity of the painful feelings of grief that they are experiencing. And, as a result of growing feelings of independence, teenagers don't want to accept adult help in coping with these feelings. Yet as with children, adult support and understanding during this time is critical.

Unique Environmental Conditions

Adults assume that when a death occurs, adolescents are surrounded by supportive family and friends. In reality, this situation may not be true at all. The lack of available support often make adults place inappropriate social expectations on bereaved teens. Teenagers, for example, are expected to be grown-up and responsible for caring for others in the family, particularly a surviving parent or younger brothers and sisters. When this occurs, teenagers do not give themselves, nor are they given, permission to mourn.

While regressive behavior is a normal response to the death, sometimes adolescents are openly encouraged to be hypermature and accept responsibility far beyond their years. Like children, teenagers fall into the "Big-Man" and "Big-Woman" syndrome. The result is a repression of mourning for the adolescent and the possibility of a delayed grief response later in life.

Another unique environmental condition experienced by bereaved adolescents involves the changing nature of family life today. Historically, the extended family offered understanding during times of distress. The teenager could turn to aunts or uncles for support.

Today, however, over fifty million Americans move each year. This mobility makes it more difficult for families to reach out to one another for understanding. Such a fast-paced, mobile culture results in increased isolation for teenagers when someone loved dies. In addition, peers often provide little or no support to grieving teenagers. Their grief is often met with indifference, except in circumstances in which a friend has also experienced the death of a family member. More typically, however, peers choose to ignore the subject of loss entirely.

Potential of Conflicting Relationships

As teenagers move toward independence, relationship conflicts are common. A normal, although trying, way teens separate from parents is by going through a period of "devaluation." If a parent, however, dies while the teenager is pushing the parent away, the teenager often experiences a heightened sense of guilt. While the need to create this distance is healthy, it complicates the experience of mourning for adolescents.

A majority of this conflict between teenagers and parents comes from the normal process of forming independent identities and values. Death combined with the turbulence of this relationship often makes it critical for the adolescent to talk about what the relationship was like before the parent died.

Another factor that influences a teenager's complications with grief is the heightened sense of ambivalence the teen feels about his or her parents. Adolescence is sometimes commensurate with parental love-hate relationships. If the parent dies, talking about this ambivalence seems essential to doing the work of mourning. Unfortunately, many teen-agers do not have an adult in their lives with whom they can have such a conversation. A relationship based on trust is required.

In contrast, a teenager may have the opposite of an ambivalent relationship with a parent. Instead, the teen may be hyperdependent. This is particularly true for adolescents with poor social or communications skills who have difficulty creating and maintaining meaningful peer relationships. If the parent dies, the teenager often experiences a total sense of isolation and hopelessness.

Conflicting relationships for teenagers also occur with boyfriends and girlfriends. If a conflict is in progress when the death occurs, the adolescent may be left with a feeling of unfinished business. Or the teen may feel guilty for the death. In such circumstances, these teenagers can be at risk of committing suicide and, as a result, require special attention.

Consequences of Postponed Mourning in the Adolescent

The specific reasons bereaved adolescents have difficulty with mourning in healthy ways are multiple and complicated. Major roadblocks stand in their way. The most common consequences of this complicated grief process among teenagers are:

- ◆ Symptoms of chronic depression, sleeping difficulties, restlessness and low self-esteem.
- ◆ Academic failure or general indifference to school-related activities.
- ◆ Deterioration in relationships with family and friends, often leading to trouble forming intimate relationships in adulthood.
- ◆ Acting out in a variety of ways: drug and

alcohol abuse, fighting and inappropriate risk-taking and sexual behavior.

◆ Denial of grief with an accompanying demonstration of hypermaturity.

◆ Symptoms of chronic anxiety and agitation.

A Final Note About Adolescent Mourning

When reviewing the possible negative influences that may affect a bereaved teenager, it is imperative that caring adults be supportive and understanding during this difficult time. Experiencing the death of a loved one is never easy, no matter what the age of the survivor. But the adolescent years hold a particular challenge and require a concerted effort by adults to help the teenager do the work of mourning.

Final Thoughts About Children and Grief

For children, the journey through grief is complex. And each child's journey is unique. Caring adults need to communicate to children that these feelings are not something to be ashamed of or to hide. Instead, grief is a natural expression of love for the person who has died.

As caring adults, the challenge is clear; children do not choose between grieving and not grieving; adults, on the other hand, do have a choice — to help or not to help children cope with grief.

As demonstrated by reading this booklet, your choice is obviously to help. Congratulations on expanding your knowledge of this important subject. Hopefully, this experience will be just a beginning, and you will continue to build your awareness through additional grief education. Inspire others to do the same.

With education, plus love and understanding, "helping-healing" adults can guide children through this vulnerable time and make it a valuable part of children's personal growth and development.

Selected Bibliography

Bernstein, J. (1977). *Books to Help Children Cope With Separation and Loss* New York, NY: R. R. Bowker

Furman, E. (1974). *A Child's Parent Dies: Studies in Childhood Bereavement* New Haven, CT: Yale University Press

Gordon, A. and Klass, D. (1979). *They Need to Know: How to Teach Children About Death* Englewood Cliffs, NJ: Prentice-Hall

Grollman, E. (Ed.) (1967). *Explaining Death to Children* Boston, MA: Beacon

Jackson, E. (1965). *Telling a Child About Death* New York, NY: Hawthorn

LeShan, E. (1980). *Learning to Say Goodbye: When a Parent Dies* New York, NY: Springer

Lonetto, R. (1980). *Children's Conceptions of Death* New York, NY: Springer

Wass, H. and Corr, C. (1982). *Helping Children Cope With Death: Guidelines and Resources* New York, NY: Hemisphere/McGraw Hill

Wass, H. and Corr, C. (Eds.) (1983). *Childhood and Death* Washington, DC: Hemisphere/McGraw Hill

Wolfelt, A. (1983). *Helping Children Cope With Grief* Muncie, IN: Accelerated Development

Wolfelt, A. (1986). "Death and Grief in the School Setting", *Crisis Intervention Strategies for School Based Helpers* Springfield, IL: Charles C. Thomas

Wolfelt, A. (1987). Brochure—*Helping Children Cope With Grief* Fort Collins, CO: Center For Loss and Life Transition

Wolfelt, A. (1988). "Bereavement and Children: Questions, Funerals, and Explaining Religious Beliefs" *Bereavement,* Vol 2. No. 1, January, pp. 16-17

Wolfelt, A. (1989). "Factors That Influence Acting-Out in Bereaved Children" *Bereavement,* Vol 3. No. 5, June, pp. 18-19 ◆

The Professional Resource

Alan Wolfelt, Ph.D. is a noted author, teacher, and practicing clinical thanatologist. He serves as director of The Center for Loss and Life Transition in Fort Collins, Colorado, and is on the faculty at the University of Colorado Medical School in the Department of Family Medicine. He is known internationally for his outstanding educational contributions in both adult and childhood grief.

Dr. Wolfelt serves as an educational consultant to hospices, hospitals, schools, universities, funeral homes, and a variety of community agencies. In 1983, he completed a fellowship in the Department of Psychiatry and Psychology at the Mayo Clinic.

A respected author, Dr. Wolfelt serves as the editor of the "Children and Grief" department of *Bereavement* magazine, and is a regular contributor to the journal *Thanatos*. Among his books are *Helping Children Cope With Grief, Death and Grief: A Guide For Clergy,* and *Interpersonal Skills Training: A Handbook for Funeral Home Staffs.* He is currently authoring a new book titled *Grief and Mourning: A Handbook for Mental Health Personnel.*